Augmented Reality

Growth in businesses in the early days of spatial computing.

Epris E. Ezekiel

Copyright 2024© Epris E. Ezekiel
All rights reserved. This book is copyrighted and no part of it may be reproduced, distributed, or transmitted in any form or by any means, including photocopying, recording, or other electronic or mechanical methods, without the prior written permission of the publisher, except in the case of brief quotations embodied in critical reviews and certain other non-commercial uses permitted by copyright law.
Printed in the United States of America Copyright 2024© Epris E. Ezekiel

Contents

Introduction 1

Chapter 1 2

History 2

Chapter 2 10

How Does Augmented Reality Work? 10

Chapter 3 15

The Challenges and Solutions for Augmented Reality AR 15

Chapter 4 21

Benefits of Using Augmented Reality 21

Chapter 5 30

Applications in Augmented Reality 30

Chapter 6 43

The Impact of Augmented Reality 43

Chapter 7 48

How Do You Integrate Augmented Reality into Your Business?
.... 48

Conclusion 51

Introduction

We are in an exciting new world of technology, with augmented reality becoming a part of our daily lives. AR's success stems from its early adoption by tech titans like Google, Apple, and Microsoft. While Apple announced ARKit in 2017, Google released its web API in the same year. Apple AR glasses are another significant advancement in the AR field.

Augmented reality (AR) allows the real-time integration of computer-generated images into the physical world. AR apps use your device's camera and sensors to establish your location and what to show you. Even if you've never heard of augmented reality, you've most likely seen it in action. While augmented reality technology may appear difficult initially, it is far more fascinating and overwhelming to experience. If you're curious about augmented reality, why it exists, and how it works, you've come to the correct spot. The well-known game Pokémon Go is one example. Other examples are TikTok and Snapchat filters. In this essay, we will define augmented reality (AR), explain how it works, and show you some instances.

Chapter 1

History

In the 1990s and early 2000s, AR research and development continued to grow, leading to several significant breakthroughs:

The "Virtual Fixtures" system was developed in 1991 as technology continued to evolve. This system allowed a user to interact with a 3D virtual environment using a glove and a haptic feedback device.

First industrial in 1992: Tom Caudell and David Mizell created this program to help factory workers assemble components more efficiently.

In 1998, academics at the University of North Carolina developed AR Toolkit, an open-source software framework that made AR creation more accessible.

With the increased availability of smartphones and mobile devices in the 2010s, augmented reality gained popularity and accessibility to a larger audience. This resulted in an explosion of AR development and application across a variety of industries, including gaming, retail, and education.

Niantic launched the augmented reality game "Ingress" in 2012, which served as the foundation for the massively popular "Pokemon Go" AR game in 2016.

People may now experience augmented reality on their phones and tablets thanks to advancements in mobile technology, AR-based apps, and software. This allows users to examine 3D objects and landscapes while also providing interactive components like tutorials and games.

The technology is evolving, with businesses like Microsoft and Apple investing considerably in AR research and development. In 2019, Apple unveiled its first commercially accessible AR device, the iPhone 11 Pro, which supported a variety of AR-based apps and experiences.

Current Status of Augmented Reality

Augmented reality has gone a long way and holds enormous promise. It has progressed from a science-fiction concept to a reality, with hardware and software engineers working to improve the technology. Gaming, the military, industry, and medicine are just a handful of the current uses for augmented reality. Gatwick Airport, for example, uses them to help passengers traverse the airport. On a more personal level, AR programs like Wikitude and IKEA Place enable users to perceive numerous objects and situations.

As developers regularly produce and deploy new advancements and apps, augmented reality (AR) improves and expands its capabilities. IDC expects the worldwide augmented reality business to approach $120 billion by 2023.

In general, augmented reality is becoming increasingly integrated into our daily lives, allowing us to bridge the gap between the real and virtual worlds while increasing efficiency, productivity, and teamwork. Because of its myriad potential applications, experts believe that augmented reality will become even more popular.

What are the various types of augmented reality?

There are two forms of augmented reality utilized for business purposes. Depending on your needs, you can opt to construct an AR experience in one of the following:

1. **Markerless AR**

    Marker-less AR creates an AR experience by starting with a surface. An augmented reality experience is created by overlaying digital elements on top of the surface.

    You will not require a physical marker to initiate an AR encounter in the real world. An AR program uses GPS, a compass, and an accelerometer to recognize the surrounding area. It also identifies real-world elements such as color and pattern, allowing virtual objects to be placed within the actual environment. A trial of a painting on the wall can be used to demonstrate markerless AR.

2. Marker-based AR

Marker-based AR employs photos as markers. Digital materials like as 3D models, photos, movies, and animation clips are superimposed over the marker to create an augmented reality experience. Scanning the QR code in WebAR allows you to watch the AR experience by pointing toward the marker.

To use mobile AR, you must first install the AR app. When you point to the marker, an AR experience will appear.

You can see the digital elements and photographs in more detail. You may also rotate the AR experience to view objects from various perspectives.

Markerless AR is classified into four types:

Contour-based AR:

This sort of AR employs specialized technology that makes use of your device's camera to create borders for objects you encounter. It is very popular for locating items in low-visibility situations.

Overlay AR:

As the name implies, "Overlay AR" masks real-world items with virtual objects, allowing the human eye to see only the replacement image with additional digital content.

Projection-based AR:

Projection-based augmented reality operates within a static space and can only present AR experiences in projected locations. So, you will only be able to witness the experience if the physical surface on which you want to superimpose a digital object is inside the area where your device camera projects.

Location-based Augmented Reality:

This markerless AR leverages your smartphone's GPS, compass, and accelerometer to locate physical space and place virtual items. As a result, even if the surface on which you want to display an augmented object moves, you may still view the experience. Furthermore, location-based AR works in various distinct ways:

1. Area-based AR, unlike surface-based AR, does not allow you to watch the experience from any surface. To create augmented digital content, you must point to the target location.

2. Surface-based - By directing your device's camera to a surface, you can observe the experience.

What's the difference between Augmented Reality, Virtual Reality, and Mixed Reality?

AR (Augmented Reality), VR (Virtual Reality), and MR

(Mixed Reality) are all related technologies, but they differ in how they integrate the digital and physical worlds.

. **AR** augments the real world with digital information and elements while preserving the physical environment in most cases. The digital content is layered on the physical environment and is intended to improve it.

. **VR** generates an entirely simulated environment that replaces the actual world. Users wear a headset that covers their eyes and provides an immersive experience, fully isolating them from the physical world.

. **MR** connects the physical and digital worlds, allowing for interaction between both. It is more immersive than augmented reality but less than virtual reality. In MR, digital content is attached to the physical world, giving the impression that it is part of the surroundings.

In brief, AR enriches the real world with digital content, VR replaces the actual world with a digital environment, and MR combines the physical and digital worlds to enable interaction.

Chapter 2

How Does Augmented Reality Work?

Have you ever wished you could see how something would appear in your home before purchasing it? Have you ever wondered how a particular product works without having to open the package? This is now possible because of augmented reality (AR). AR technology enhances the existing world by adding information on top of it. This can take the shape of 3D objects, audio, text, or GPS data.

Technical Explanation of how Augmented Reality works about Computer Vision

Augmented reality (AR) produces a 3D experience that enables users to engage with both the physical and digital worlds by superimposing digital data onto real-world items. An augmented reality device, such as smart glasses, a tablet, or a smartphone, can parse a video stream to identify real-world objects or the user's surroundings. After connecting to a digital twin - a 3D digital representation of an object stored in the cloud - in both real and virtual environments, the device retrieves information about the object from the cloud and superimposes digital data on it.

Two components of computer vision techniques are used to do this:

1. The initial stage in identifying interest spots, fiducial markers, or optical flow in camera images is to use various image processing techniques, such as corner detection, blob detection, edge detection, thresholding, and other feature identification approaches.

2. In the second stage, the system uses the information gathered in the previous step to reconstruct a real-world coordinate system. This stage entails either using SLAM (Simultaneous Localization and Mapping), structure from motion techniques such as bundle adjustment, or assuming the presence of objects with known geometry (or fiducial markers) in the scene. Projective (epipolar) geometry, geometric

algebra, exponential map-based rotation representation, Kalman and particle filters, nonlinear optimization, and robust statistics are also used.

Augmented Reality Devices: Hardware and Software

To experience augmented reality (AR), a user requires both hardware and software components.

The hardware components of AR systems are:

- ✓ Projectors may project virtual images onto real-world surfaces or objects.

- ✓ AR contact lenses are wearable devices that blend augmented reality technology into contact lenses, allowing users to see digital information right in their field of vision.

- ✓ Projectors may project virtual images onto real-world surfaces or objects.

- ✓ AR glasses, which are smaller and more wearable than HMDs, are comparable products.

- ✓ Many AR applications are accessible through mobile devices such as smartphones and tablets, which have built-in cameras, screens, and processing capabilities.

- ✓ Users use headsets or head-mounted displays (HMDs) to see virtual pictures superimposed on the actual world.

The software components of AR systems are:

- ❖ **AR Browsers:** These are specialized browsers that enable users to view and interact with augmented reality material on the web.

- ❖ **AR Development Software: This** is used to create Augmented Reality applications and experiences. Examples include ARKit and ARCore.

- **AR Content Management Systems (CMS):** These platforms manage and organize AR content, making it easier to develop and share AR experiences.

To summarize, AR involves both hardware and software components to provide users with an improved and augmented experience. The specific hardware and software components required are determined by the specific AR application and experience being built.

Chapter 3

The Challenges and Solutions for Augmented Reality AR

Augmented Reality (AR) is changing how we interact with the world around us by superimposing digital information on our actual environs. AR has many possible uses, including retail, education, healthcare, and entertainment. However, like with any growing technology, substantial challenges exist. In this piece of writing, we'll look at the fundamental problems of augmented reality AR creation and propose new ideas to assist overcome them.

Market Adoption Challenges

1. **Consumer Awareness and Understanding** Increasing public awareness and understanding of AR's benefits is critical for mainstream adoption. Many potential consumers remain unaware of how AR can be used in their daily lives or enterprises.

Possible solutions

Effective marketing methods, such as instructional content and real-world examples, can assist close the knowledge gap. An Augmented Reality Development Company in India could hold workshops and live demos to demonstrate the potential of AR.

2. **Cost Implications**

   The high expenses of developing and deploying augmented reality systems can be a substantial barrier to entry for many enterprises.

   Possible Solutions

   Creating low-cost AR solutions and implementing scalable, as-a-service models can help make AR more accessible to a wider range of enterprises and customers.

Privacy and Security Challenges

1. **Security vulnerabilities**

   The networked structure of AR applications makes them susceptible to security vulnerabilities. These vulnerabilities have the potential to expose user data and allow unwanted access to personal information.

   Possible Solutions

   A thorough security approach, including regular updates, patches, and secure coding techniques, is required to protect AR apps. To secure its consumers, an Augmented Reality Development Company must emphasize these security standards.

2. **Data Privacy Concerns**

   AR apps often acquire and handle large amounts of personal data to work properly, raising serious privacy concerns. Ensuring that user data is handled securely is critical.

Possible Solutions

Implementing strong data protection methods, such as strong encryption and safe data storage techniques, is critical. Transparency in data usage and providing users control over their information are also necessary approaches.

User Experience Challenges

1. **Latency and Real-Time Processing**

    actual-time processing is required for AR experiences to smoothly overlay digital information onto the actual world. Delays or latency can degrade the user experience and reduce the technology's effectiveness.

    Possible Solutions

    Optimizing software to reduce latency and implementing more powerful processing technologies are critical measures. Furthermore, edge computing can be used to process data closer to its source, minimizing delays.

2. **Physical and Digital Content Alignment**
   Achieving the perfect alignment of digital content with the physical world is critical for delivering a credible AR experience. This alignment is difficult due to the dynamic nature of real-world situations.

   Possible Solutions
   Advanced tracking and spatial recognition technologies are essential. Incorporating artificial intelligence into these processes can result in improved alignment and a more immersive AR experience.

3. **Accessibility and Inclusion**
   Another big problem is making AR technologies accessible to people with all abilities. AR apps must be created with inclusivity in mind, allowing users of various physical and sensory abilities.

Possible Solutions

Accessibility should be prioritized from the start while developing augmented reality. This includes adhering to established accessibility criteria and consulting with varied user groups throughout the design process to ensure broad usability.

Chapter 4

Benefits of Using Augmented Reality

The challenges of augmented reality are now obvious. But what advantages does this technology provide us in overcoming them? AR can improve many parts of our lives, including the way we shop and learn. The possible uses are numerous and are only limited by human imagination.

1. **Obtain more accurate results.**

    Augmented reality aids in obtaining more accurate findings by visually providing context, step-by-step comparison, communication, and validation via a portable device or even a wearable device such as Microsoft HaloLens, RealWear, and others. This out-of-the-box technology enables technicians to access senior technicians' knowledge at their fingertips via a smartphone or tablet, reducing ambiguity in context when 3D digital content is superimposed on top of the product itself.

This allows users to examine the physical product and get the information they need right away, resulting in better maintenance and workforce training, a higher first-time fix rate (FTFR), and less customer downtime. AR also gives a form of X-ray vision, displaying inside details that would otherwise be difficult to view, considerably increasing the success rate of medical procedures.

2. **Reach a wider audience.**
    - ✓ Provide access to digital content without the need for additional equipment

    - ✓ Enables remote demonstrations and training.

    - ✓ Offer unique and memorable marketing tactics.

    - ✓ Showcase products in a virtual setting.

    - ✓ Offer interactive and interesting experiences.

3. **Have More Fun**
    - ✓ Interact with virtual characters and items in real-world environments.
    - ✓ Discover fresh and engaging experiences with AR tours and adventures.
    - ✓ Play AR games.
    - ✓ Enhance your photo/video experience with AR filters and effects.
    - ✓ Bring digital material to life in physical environments.

4. **Enhance understanding and comprehension**

Augmented reality (AR) can dramatically improve knowledge and comprehension by providing real-time, step-by-step visual instruction on operations like product assembly, machine operation, and warehouse picking. AR can eliminate ambiguity in context by superimposing 3-D digital content on top of a physical product, allowing inspectors to see the physical product and get the information they require.

AR can also enhance worker training and performance by delivering interactive 3-D holograms that guide users through the necessary processes, removing the need for costly and time-consuming 2-D schematic representations seen in manuals. Furthermore, firms can use augmented reality (AR) to accelerate training and close employee skill gaps by putting senior technicians' knowledge at their fingertips via mobile devices. Thus, augmented reality can be used to improve learning opportunities, reduce maintenance downtime, and, ultimately, improve understanding and comprehension.

5. **Save time and effort.**

    Augmented reality (AR) can assist save time and effort by enhancing workforce training and performance, increasing new hire productivity, raising first-time repair rates, accelerating sales, lowering training costs, and lowering scrap and rework expenses. AR-guided instructions provide visual context, step-by-step comparison, and confirmation, allowing for first-time maintenance. AR also puts senior technicians' knowledge at their fingertips via a smartphone or tablet, while remote servicing reduces the need for travel, saving hours, days, and even weeks. AR-enabled instructions can empower frontline workers to improve quality while driving continuous improvement.

6. **Improve Your Productivity**

    ✓ Reduce errors and improve accuracy in tasks.

    ✓ Provide hands-free operation to promote mobility.

    ✓ Improve communication and teamwork.

    ✓ Improve visual aids to help with tasks.

    ✓ Streamline information access and display.

7. **Experience Augmented Reality in Your Way.** Wearing AR glasses or a headset allows for a full

experience that includes sound, touch, and even smell. This can transform one's immediate surroundings into an interactive learning space. Retailers and other businesses can utilize augmented reality to promote their products or services, launch new marketing initiatives, and collect personalized customer data. Furthermore, AR may be used in the workplace to improve business outcomes and differentiate brands, allowing industrial users to get more familiar with their systems and machines while also optimizing and augmenting technology and IoT networks.

8. **Get Closer to Reality.**

Augmented reality (AR) can bridge the gap between our physical and digital worlds, allowing us to make better use of the massive amounts of data available to us. By superimposing digital information and images on actual objects and settings, we can obtain a much better awareness of the context in which we are functioning, allowing us to act on this data in real-time. This technology is already being used in a range of applications, including product development, logistics, marketing, and training, to provide people with new ways to perceive information, receive and follow instructions, and interact with products.

AccuVein, for example, has used augmented reality technology to convert a patient's vein heat signature into a superimposed image on their skin, making them much easier to find. Similarly, Boeing has used AR to reduce the time it takes trainees to assemble an aircraft wing by 35%, and factories are incorporating voice commands into AR experiences to help workers perform complex wiring more quickly and accurately.

These examples highlight AR's ability to improve productivity and accuracy in a wide range of industries, empowering enterprises to make their processes more effective and their workforce more educated. AR might be a game changer for businesses trying to boost engagement and consumer loyalty and those looking to give their employees an advantage in an increasingly competitive global market.

9. **Access more information Easily**

    Augmented Reality (AR) enables consumers to obtain more information more quickly by providing powerful self-help and support options, real-time access to essential information, and critical information layered on the physical product under inspection. AR also reduces downtime due to malfunctioning equipment, improves maintenance and training, and improves customer experiences by increasing consumer search with features such as the ability to identify things, inform the user what the text says, and even record critical numbers.

10. **Improve Your View of the World**

    AR has the potential to dramatically revolutionize how we perceive the world.

- ✓ AR connects us to multimedia content, allowing us to view images, movies, and graphics that enhance our surroundings.
- ✓ Augmented reality, which displays visual and geographical information, allows us to better understand our surroundings, as well as the objects and people in it. This is especially useful for navigation, as AR can provide clear, thorough instructions.
- ✓ AR, which combines physical and digital components, can provide us with access to information that we would not otherwise have.

Applications in Augmented Reality

There are numerous ways in which businesses are employing augmented reality to improve the way we interact with the world, ranging from education and entertainment to advertising, gaming, and even healthcare.

Chapter 5

Applications in Augmented Reality

There are numerous ways in which businesses are employing augmented reality to improve the way we interact with the world, ranging from education and entertainment to advertising, gaming, and even healthcare.

1. **Automotive and Transportation**

   AR can help industrial designers see and change automobile body structure and engine arrangement by allowing them to experience the design and operation of a product before it is completed. Volkswagen used augmented reality to compare digital and physical crash test images, detecting anomalies. Furthermore, augmented reality (AR) can aid in the analysis, evaluation, and enhancement of 3-D designs, as well as the comparison of computer-aided design (CAD) models to physical prototypes.

   In manufacturing, AR can assist to eliminate errors and improve production efficiency by presenting the relevant information to industrial workers at the right time. AR can also capture data from automation and control systems, secondary sensors, and asset management systems, making critical monitoring and diagnostic data visible. AR interfaces provide for more efficient monitoring of machines and processes, as well as the ability to link essential information to the physical location where it will be most easily viewed, hence reducing costly downtime and increasing productivity.

AR can also be utilized in logistics and warehouses to improve picking efficiency. AR-based instructions and guidance can assist workers in rapidly and accurately locating objects, saving time and eliminating errors associated with manual searches. Furthermore, augmented reality may provide specific product information and stock-level data, making warehouse management more efficient and cost-effective.

2. **Lifestyle**

   What lifestyle augmented reality applications are available? Augmented reality has a wide range of potential lifestyle applications, including assisting with home decorating and design using IKEA's AR App, providing information on various destinations and points of interest using travel apps, providing information on products and services via shopping apps, and providing interactive learning experiences. Augmented reality can also be utilized for enjoyment, such as playing interactive games, viewing movies, and taking virtual tours.

3. **Social Media**

   Augmented reality in social media can provide users with exciting, unique experiences. Users of augmented reality apps can now interact with products and services in previously impractical ways. Snapchat, for example, is a social networking software that allows users to apply special effects and filters to their photos and videos using augmented reality. Brands can create their custom Snapchat filters and use them to promote their products.

Other popular AR applications include iOS and Android apps that let users add 3D objects to images and videos, as well as utilize their phones to preview things before purchasing them. Brands can also offer personalized experiences that show customers how their products will seem in their home or office setting.

Brands may employ AR in social media to create interesting, interactive experiences for consumers, thereby strengthening their brand, increasing demand, and shortening sales cycles. AR applications provide users with a multidimensional approach to studying and interacting with products and services, making the experience more fun and engaging.

4. **Advertising & Marketing**

Marketing and advertising can use augmented reality to provide clients with an involved and interesting experience. AR allows businesses to present their products in new and inventive ways, which can increase consumer engagement and revenue.

AR in advertising includes the usage of AR-enabled billboards, which allow users to interact with virtual goods and promotions in real time. As a result, customers may have a more compelling and long-lasting experience with advertising.

Another use of augmented reality in marketing is in print media, such as magazines and newspapers. Customers can scan print ads with AR-enabled devices to get additional content such as videos, product data, and more. Augmented reality can also help to improve in-store experiences by providing customers with additional information and interesting activities. Customers may obtain a virtual tour of a store, replete with product data and discounts, through an AR application, for example.

5. **Travel**

   Travelers can utilize AR to view real-time informational displays about a site, including its features and comments or content left by past visitors. Advanced AR apps can also show passengers simulations of historical events, places, and items that have been placed into the landscape. In the Netherlands, cell phone owners can download an application that uses their phone's camera and GPS to gather information about their surroundings.

   Furthermore, organizations such as Mural Arts Philadelphia have built interactive outdoor murals that visitors may explore with their smartphones. Finally, apps like Augment and AR Compass Map 3D can provide passengers with a visual of things they might be interested in purchasing or a 3D map to help them get to their destination.

6. **Gaming and Entertainment.**

   Users can access a wide range of leisure and gaming alternatives. These include augmented reality field hockey, augmented reality billiards games, and Titans of Space, a cooperative fight with artificially intelligent opponents. Games like Halo: King of the Hill, NBA: King of the Court, and Paranormal Activity: Sanctuary uses augmented reality to allow for location-based gameplay. AR may be used in mobile games like Star Wars: Jedi Challenges and Pokémon Go to create immersive gaming experiences. ARGs (augmented reality games) promote movies and television shows on a variety of media.

7. **Healthcare and medicine**

   Augmented reality is becoming increasingly popular in healthcare and medicine for a variety of applications:

   ✓ Viewing a fetus inside a mother's womb.

- ✓ Guiding diagnostic and therapeutic interventions, such as surgery.

- ✓ Visualizing tumor position, radiation exposure hazards, and subsurface tumors and veins during surgery.

- ✓ The near-infrared vein finder can discover veins.

- ✓ Reminding people to take their meds

- ✓ Cockroach and spider phobia therapy

- ✓ Virtual X-ray view based on previous tomography or real-time pictures from ultrasound and confocal microscopy probes.

8. **Education & Training**

    Augmented reality (AR) offers students and trainees a more immersive and dynamic learning experience by allowing them to interact in real-time with virtual objects, simulations, and real-life scenarios.

    Virtual field trips are one example of augmented reality in education. Students can utilize AR devices to explore virtual environments such as museums, historical places, and other locales to learn about history, science, and other subjects.

    Another application of AR in education is the use of simulations to provide hands-on learning opportunities. Students, for example, can employ augmented reality simulations to better learn complex scientific concepts in topics like biology, chemistry, and physics. AR can improve learning outcomes by allowing students to practice skills in virtual surroundings. Students could use augmented reality (AR) to perform medical operations, military drills, or firefighting skills without risking their lives or incurring the expenditures of real-world training.

In conclusion, augmented reality has the potential to improve educational and training experiences by offering a more immersive and engaging mode of learning.

9. Construction and Architecture

Augmented reality (AR) is increasingly being used in construction and architecture to visualize building projects, improve workspaces, and enhance tourist attractions. AR enables the superimposition of computer-generated images of constructions onto real-world local views before their construction. It can also create animated 3D visualizations and allow users to peek through outside walls to observe inner plans. Businesses are also employing augmented reality to view georeferenced models of construction sites, underground infrastructure, cables, and pipes via mobile devices.

AR has a variety of applications, like the introduction of CityViewAR following the Christchurch earthquake to view ruined structures. AR systems are also collaborative design and planning tools, allowing you to create augmented reality maps and superimpose designs and plans in the real environment. Smart city initiatives use augmented reality to increase operational efficiency and public service quality.

Finally, augmented reality (AR) aids archaeological study by superimposing elements onto modern environments, allowing archaeologists to evaluate excavation results and offering 3D panoramic photos and site models.

10. **Retail and E-commerce**

Augmented reality (AR) is increasingly becoming a valuable tool for retailers and e-commerce businesses. Approximately 48% of consumers are interested in using AR and other metaverse technologies for shopping in the next five years, while 38% of marketers have already used AR to engage customers online and in-store. AR has a variety of uses for e-commerce and retail firms, allowing clients to experience mass customization and other features remotely. It can be used in a variety of ways to give customers a more immersive, interactive, and enjoyable purchasing experience.

- ❖ Home Shopping: Before making a purchase, shoppers may virtually place furniture in their living spaces to see how it will fit and seem.

- ❖ In-store purchasing experience: More information and engaging activities. Customers, for example, can be provided a virtual tour of the business using an AR application, which includes product information and discounts.

- ❖ Customers can use their smartphones to learn more about a product, such as its ingredients, nutritional information, or manufacturer.

❖ Virtual try-on experiences allow customers to see how a product will look on them in real-time without having to physically put it on. This is particularly important for things such as apparel and accessories, as it allows buyers to make more educated purchasing decisions.

Overall, augmented reality has the potential to alter retail and e-commerce by offering customers a more immersive and participatory buying experience. The application of augmented reality in various industries is ever-changing, with new technology and solutions being developed all the time.

Chapter 6

The Impact of Augmented Reality

The impact of augmented reality on society is profound and far-reaching, with both advantages and disadvantages. From education and entertainment to healthcare and industry, AR has the potential to change the way we work, study, and play. We'll look at how augmented reality is affecting society and what it could mean for the future.

Ethical considerations

The ethical implications for augmented reality are numerous and complicated. On the one hand, the device's constant recording capability may result in privacy infringement. Legal issues may occur, particularly in regions where a certain level of privacy is required, or where copyrighted media is displayed. In addition, the Code of Ethics on Human Augmentation was ratified, to protect users from the exploitation of their data and information.

In contrast, UX design can improve people's daily lives. This encompasses factors including safety, overkill, environmental impact, comfort, security, and accessibility. There is also the problem of achieving metaverse interoperability and recognizing the implications for the future of employment. Furthermore, developers must evaluate the main metaverse cybersecurity concerns and how to overcome them. All of these factors must be considered when developing an AR experience to guarantee that users are not put in danger and that their data is protected.

Environmental impact

Augmented reality can have a positive impact on the environment by improving users' perceptions of the world and making them more visually appealing. AR technology can help to minimize pollution and promote sustainability by developing digital overlays that blend seamlessly with the physical world. However, there is fear that over-reliance on AR systems may cause users to ignore critical environmental cues, resulting in accidents, injuries, and increased expenditures. As a result, it is critical to strike a balance between using AR technology to improve our environment and staying aware of our surroundings to safeguard our safety and well-being.

Economic Impact

Augmented reality (AR) has a big economic impact. AR technology helps organizations increase their profitability by increasing staff productivity and safety, enhancing operational performance, and cutting expenses in factories and on the field. AR is also useful for distributed team communication through conferences with both local and virtual participants, as well as machine assembly and maintenance. It even helps workers improve their skills and efficiency.

The digital revolution, powered by AR and other technologies, is increasing productivity and value across the economy. However, it is also creating concerns about human opportunity, with some claiming that new technology would reduce it. However, in the past, new technologies have frequently resulted in increased employment.

Overall, augmented reality is transforming the economy by increasing efficiency, unlocking value, and generating new sorts of jobs and services. Humans still have particular strengths that robots and algorithms cannot imitate, therefore humans continue to play an important role in the economy.

Social Impact

Augmented reality has a two-fold social influence. On the one hand, it has the potential to improve workplace cooperation, boost productivity, and unlock value throughout the economy. However, it raises worries about human opportunity, as the rapid progress of machine learning and automation threatens to replace human labor.
AR has been used to help remote teams collaborate and enhance industrial operations. It can also increase worker productivity in a variety of jobs, even without prior training. It can improve workers' skills and efficiency, resulting in increased economic growth and better jobs.

At the same time, the rise of artificial intelligence and

robots may result in job displacement. However, history has demonstrated that new technology frequently leads to the emergence of previously unimaginable types of jobs. As a result, it is critical to acknowledge humans' distinct assets, such as dexterity and motor skills, which no computer or algorithm can imitate. These abilities can be utilized to perform both subtle manipulation jobs and less skilled activities, such as taking blood or mending a flat tire. If used correctly, AR can be a vital tool for people to maximize their potential and secure their continued inclusion in the future of work.

Chapter 7

How Do You Integrate Augmented Reality into Your Business?

Businesses utilizing augmented reality adhere to a defined plan, ensuring a systematic and effective integration. This strategic strategy ensures that augmented reality solutions are seamlessly integrated with company objectives and contribute to long-term success. It entails meticulous planning, exact implementation strategies, and ongoing evaluation.

Steps to Integrate Augmented Reality in Your Business

Conduct market research.

Rather than following the hype, you must delve deeper into your business industry and comprehend the potential of technology. You must invest time and effort in the augmented reality market and competitive study to determine what AR may be used for, its future, and how the technology has assisted them in creating a new image in the marketplace.

Determine Use Cases.

Analyze the potential applications of augmented reality in the industry. Determine where augmented reality could provide value and solve specific challenges, ranging from consumer interactions to business operations.

Analyze technological requirements.

Consider the technologies required for AR integration, including hardware, software, and prospective collaborations. Check compatibility with existing systems and infrastructure.

Create an Integration Strategy.

Create a detailed plan outlining how augmented reality will help your company's goals. Consider money, schedule, and scalability to ensure successful implementation.

Choose AR Platforms.

Determine which AR platforms or technologies are best suited to your business's needs. Choose platforms that help you achieve your goals, whether you use pre-existing apps or create your own.

Create user-friendly experiences.

In augmented reality apps, user experience should be prioritized. Provide user-friendly interfaces and engaging information to provide a smooth user experience.

Test and iterate

Put augmented reality apps through rigorous testing in real-world environments. To improve performance and address any issues, solicit feedback and iterate on functionality and design.

Monitor and analyze

To monitor and collect data about AR usage, tracking systems should be put in place. Examine performance indicators about specified goals and, where necessary, change based on facts.

Conclusion

AR has several applications, including conveying environmental data and generating immersive game worlds. There are many possibilities, and as technology progresses, we can only expect to see even more amazing augmented-reality applications in the future.

The future of augmented reality appears promising. As technology advances, the potential uses of augmented reality become increasingly obvious. Wearable technologies could create a more immersive and fuller link between the real and virtual worlds, opening up a plethora of new possibilities. With each step ahead in the digital revolution, it becomes clear that augmented reality is and will be an important part of our lives shortly.

www.ingramcontent.com/pod-product-compliance
Lightning Source LLC
Chambersburg PA
CBHW070418230526
45471CB00006B/2872